Talk About Hope

Two Bob Hope Writers Trade Stories

by
Gene Perret
and
Martha Bolton

To Helen Romecki
Keep Smiling
Gene Perret

Jester Press
PO Box 786
Agoura Hills, CA 91376-0786

10 9 8 7 6 5 4 3 2 1

ISBN: 1-888688-02-5

Perret, Gene
Bolton, Martha
Talk about Hope: two Bob Hope writers
trade stories/Gene Perret and Martha Bolton
Humor

Edited by Anita Buck
Cover Design by Armgardt Design

Printed and bound in the United States of America
Published by Jester Press
PO Box 786
Agoura Hills, CA 91376

Contents

To Richard Eugene McMonagle
From Eugene Richard Perret

To the many talented Bob Hope writers
who've gone before us.
And to Jan, Marie, Judith, and
all the secretaries who daily made us look good.
Martha Bolton

Foreword

Two of the hottest comedy writers in the business, Gene Perret and Martha Bolton, have written a book about their boss, Bob Hope. It's an inside, back-stage look at what goes on in the highly competitive world of big-money TV comedy. And I'm thrilled to be writing their foreword. Not only because this book makes entertaining reading, not only because it's packed with laughs, not only because it's like a VIP pass to all of Bob Hope's shows, but because they might one day write a book about me.

Gene and Martha are two of my most valued friends, and they've written some of my most memorable lines. Gene once sent me a joke that said, "I'll give you an idea how bad my cooking is — last Christmas the family got together and bought me an oven that flushes." As soon as I read that joke, I knew immediately I had to have Gene as one of my writers. One of my favorite Martha Bolton lines was "I tan the easy way. I just wait for my liver spots to connect." You can see why I had to have her writing for me, too.

This book is like sitting down and having a fun chat with a couple of "pros." You'll laugh, you'll guffaw, you'll beat your chest in empathy with the dozens of stories these two leaks in security are splashing on the pages of this book.

It's no secret that I adore Rapid Robert. And by the time you finish reading this book, it won't be a secret that they do, too.

Phyllis Diller

"I hope the airlines
don't start charging us to use
the overhead compartments.
Where else would my writers sit?"

Bob Hope

Chapter One
In The Beginning. . .

My Mentor
(Gene)

When I first wanted to become a comedy writer, I was determined to learn from the best. I thought Bob Hope's material was the funniest on paper. Hope's delivery and timing always made the gags better, but still, they were funny when you read them on paper. I decided that was the kind of material I should be studying.

I would tape Bob Hope's monologues from his television specials. Then I'd type them out, analyze them, and put them away. About two weeks later I would pick new topics from the papers and write jokes about those topics using Hope's style and form. It was great training.

During my first year writing in Hollywood, Bob Hope called me. He was scheduled to emcee the Academy Awards and asked if I would try writing some gags for him.

I sat in my backyard with a notepad and pen that day and wrote 300 jokes for Bob Hope. A few days later, I watched the Academy Awards telecast. Hope used ten of my gags. I was thrilled since he only did about 30 jokes in his opening monologue.

The next day Hope called me. He said, "I loved the material you wrote for me. It looks like you've been writing for me all your life."

I said, "I have, Mr. Hope, only you didn't know about it."

We've worked together ever since.

Faith, Hope, and. . .That Late Night Call

(Martha)

A writer friend of mine was being interviewed on a local cable television station. The elderly host asked, “So, how’d you get where you are today?” My friend proceeded to explain how hard work and perseverance finally paid off. The host said, “No. I mean, how did you get here, to the studio? What freeway did you take?”

Most folks are interested in how people got where “they are today.” Not what freeway they took, but what career steps.

I cut my comedy writing teeth in the church. I was a church secretary who used to “roast” the pastor at every banquet and occasion I could. I had to keep changing churches, of course. . .

Actually, before long other churches in the community began calling me to “roast” their pastors, and I started receiving a lot of encouragement to start writing for television.

I began selling to various professional comedians, including Phyllis Diller and Joan Rivers (we share the same housekeeping and cooking techniques). But what I really wanted to do was get into scriptwriting.

Gene Perret invited me to a taping of the TV sitcom, “Mama’s Family.” He was Creative Consultant on the show, and afterwards he suggested I try writing a couple of scripts on spec. I didn’t have a typewriter that was working at the time, so for a quarter for twenty minutes of typing time, I went down to the local library and wrote a script. Gene liked my work and forwarded the script to the producer, Ed Simmons, who liked it as well. But unfortunately, the show wasn’t renewed for the new season.

Happily, the story doesn’t end there. Gene also happened to be writing for Bob Hope at the time and recommended me to him. I wrote some one-liners on several topics Hope suggested and sent them in.

Around 11:30 one night, I received a telephone call from Bob Hope. Now, you have to understand something — there was this deacon in our church who could do voices. So for the first half of the conversation, I'm responding to the compliments about my work with, "All right, Frank, knock it off. I know it's you."

Despite my skepticism, it turned out to be the real Bob Hope. Luckily, I realized that before he hung up on me. I became Bob's first woman staff writer, and after fifteen-plus years, he's still calling.

It Could Have Been a Short Career

(Gene)

I almost blew my career with Bob Hope.

When he called and asked me to write for the Academy Awards show in 1969, I told Phyllis Diller about it. She was thrilled for me, and said, "Honey, if there're any jokes of mine that you can give Bob, go right ahead."

There were a couple of jokes I had sent to Phyllis that did apply to the Oscars, so I included them in the package I sent to Hope.

Then Phyllis was asked to co-host a pre-Oscar show with Vincent Price. It was broadcast in Los Angeles on the Sunday before the Academy Awards, but in the rest of the country it was scheduled immediately before the Oscar telecast. In this show, Phyllis did a couple of the jokes that I had sent to Hope.

I panicked. What if Bob Hope and Phyllis Diller did the exact same jokes on the shows aired back to back? I was taking my family to Disneyland the next day, but I had to reach Bob Hope to explain what had happened. I called several times but couldn't reach him.

My family thought I was crazy because each time we passed a public phone at Disneyland, I'd place another call, trying to contact Bob Hope.

Finally, I got through to Mr. Hope and explained what happened. He calmly said, "Which jokes?" I read them to him and he said, "I'll take them out."

Wow, I thought. . .I hope my whole career with Bob Hope is this easy. It wasn't. Just most of it was.

On A Zing And A Prayer

(Martha)

When I first started writing for Bob Hope, my sons were ten, eight and seven years old. Being so young, I wasn't sure if they knew, really knew who it was I was writing for, who it was calling at all hours of the night.

One evening I got my answer. I walked into my middle son, Matt's, room for bedtime prayer.

He closed his eyes, folded his hands and prayed.

"Dear God, thank You for Mommy, Daddy, our dog, Chipper, our cat, my pet hamster, and thanks, Lord, for the memories."

Chapter Two

But What Have You Written for Me Lately?

The Long Wait

(Gene)

Bob Hope always wanted writers writing.

We had just finished taping a show in Tahiti and were rushing to make our flight. All of our luggage was packed and taken on ahead to be loaded onto the plane. It was a rainy evening and we had a bus ride, followed by an hour and a half ferry ride, then another bus ride to get to the airport. When we got there, we found out there was no plane for us.

Rumor had it there had been an accident in Australia that disabled one plane, and there were union problems with another airline. We were told to go back to the hotel and be ready to go to the airport for a 6 a.m. flight the next morning.

We had no luggage. Everything was packed for the flight.

The next morning, we were told there was still no plane ready for us, but to stay close to the hotel, because the call could come at any time.

It didn't come until the next day. By this time we were feeling a little gamy.

When we finally did get to the airport we had to wait in a long line outside in the hot sun. After two hours, the line had not moved at all. Again, we heard rumors — this time, that our tickets were no good and we wouldn't be allowed to board the plane.

As I stood sweating in line with one of the other writers, we watched Bob Hope's limousine pull up to the curb. We were heading back to the States, but Bob and Dolores Hope were scheduled to go on to Japan, so they were not part of this delay. Hope got out of the car looking fresh as a daisy.

He walked right over to us writers and said, "Start thinking about the Christmas show."

Taking a Breather
(Martha)

One evening while Si Jacobs, one of Bob Hope's long-time comedy writers, was eating dinner at the famous Chasen's restaurant in Beverly Hills, Bob and Dolores Hope walked in.

Si, feeling a little guilty for taking a breather from that night's assignment, said, "I'll get back to work, Bob, just as soon as I get home."

Bob Hope looked around the room and said, "What — there are no typewriters here?"

Your Choice
(Gene)

Bob Hope was always the real head writer. He was the brains behind his comedy. The writers would come up with potential topics and write tons of jokes, but Bob knew which ones were right for his act and his television shows.

Hope was doing a special at the Merv Griffin Theatre in Hollywood. He was on stage rehearsing and the writers were sitting in the audience seats observing. We were in a cluster because writers tend to band together for our own protection. It wasn't a bad idea this day.

During the rehearsal Hope read a line that got groans from

the rest of the cast and the crew. During a break, he came downstage and looked at the writers. He said, "We need a new line."

We said, "We know."

He said, "That's a terrible joke. Who wrote it?"

None of us spoke up.

Hope zeroed in on me. He said, "You wrote that, didn't you?"

I said, "Who picked it?"

Hope glared at me with that vaudeville sneer of his and said, "You're not very likable when you're right," then walked back upstage.

New Jokes Only, Please
(Martha)

When it came to material, shortcuts were something you didn't take with Bob. It was the end of the television season and Bob wanted fresh, new material for his personal appearances.

"Do some football jokes for me," he said to the writers.

Bob Mills, a terrific writer who had been with Hope for many years, knew the Hope joke files were full of football one-liners.

"Why don't you just take some old football jokes from the files?" Mills asked. "Why do we have to write new ones?"

Hope replied, "I pay you with new money, don't I?"

What Makes a Good Joke?
(Gene)

We did do a lot of football jokes for Hope.

Once another writer, Jeffrey Barron, and I traveled with Hope to Florida. We did a Christmas special down there. Every Christmas we had the All-American football team on the show. The All-Americans would be introduced one at a time. The player would come on screen, stand next to Bob Hope and do a few lines with him. That player would exit and the next one would enter for his joke.

It was no big deal for the writers because we did the same kind of joke each year. He's so big that. . . He's so fast that. . . He tackles so hard that. . .

Each of the writers would do two or three jokes for each player so we'd have plenty of one-liners to pick from when we assembled the final routine.

This year, though, Ty Detmer, a quarterback from Brigham Young University, was the Heisman Trophy winner. Bob Hope called Jeffrey and me to his suite and said he wasn't happy with any of the quarterback jokes. None of them were good enough for the Heisman Trophy winner.

So Jeff and I went back to our rooms, did about ten more gags each, and slid them under Bob Hope's door in the morning. Later in the day he said he didn't like any of those either.

We called all the writers who were back in Los Angeles and got them to write more quarterback jokes. We got another 20 or 25 jokes. Hope didn't care for those, either.

We all tried again. We must have come up with another 100 to 150 jokes before we were through. Bob Hope didn't like any of them.

Finally, about an hour before we were going to shoot this spot, Jeffrey and I went off and did some more jokes. We brought them to Hope's room, read them to him and finally got him to approve one.

I immediately wrote it into the script and got it put on cue cards — before Hope changed his mind. When it was all set, I said to Hope, "Tell me something. What makes this joke any better than the other 200 we wrote for this guy?"

Hope sneered at me and said, "I liked this one."

An Assignment to Remember
(Martha)

Our monologue assignments could be some thirty different topics on which each of us would write up to twenty jokes apiece. That's hundreds of jokes due in just a couple of days. So to make the assignment easier, we started breaking the topics into sub-topics. For example, the topic of "income taxes" would become:

1. The confusing forms
2. New ideas the government has on collecting taxes
3. Funny places our tax dollars might be going

And so on. By writing only four or five jokes per sub-topic, we'd have our twenty jokes on the subject before we knew it and could move on to the next one.

There was one time, though, when things got a little mixed up. I was supposed to pass along the assignment to writers Doug Gamble and Phil Lasker. When I called Doug to read the topics, everything went fine. But when I read them to Phil, I forgot to make the distinction between the sub-topics and the topics, so poor Phil thought they were all topics. (About seventy-five of them) requiring twenty jokes apiece. Needless to say, he didn't leave his typewriter that whole weekend.

Bob Hope didn't mind receiving all those jokes, though. He's always had an insatiable appetite for material. Once, when another writer tried to sneak by with handing in less than his usual number of jokes, Bob took the stack of papers and laid it on the palm of his hand. Then, as if weighing the jokes, he looked at the writer and said suspiciously, "You took in a movie, didn't you?"

I Wanted a COMEDY Writer

(Gene)

I always admired the way Hope could reject a joke without putting you down. In fact, he'd have a little bit of fun with it.

I remember one time I was sitting over at his house, reading one of my jokes to him. He gave me a strange look and said, "That's not very funny."

"Yeah, I know, Bob, but it has a lot of hidden meaning and people will appreciate it," I said. "If you tell that joke in front of a live audience, you'll get applause. No doubt about it."

He thought about that for a bit, then said to me, "How long have you been writing philosophy?"

No Fooling the Master
(Martha)

Once when we were working on an upcoming special, I had what I thought was a great sketch idea. Bob Hope would be the ultimate judge of that, but I was convinced it was a solid premise.

I fleshed it out as best I could, then, running out of time to meet the deadline (and frankly, running out of steam and ideas, too), I tagged on a mediocre ending. I knew it was too easy of a payoff, but I was hoping Bob wouldn't notice.

The next day at the writer's meeting, Bob flipped through the sketches, briefly commenting on each one. When he came to mine, he said, "Martha's got a funny sketch here. . . ," then proceeded to share it aloud with the group. But instead of reading my weak tag, when he got near the ending, he simply said knowingly, ". . .then Martha went to lunch."

And the Winner Is. . .
(Gene)

I was working on "The Carol Burnett Show" while I was also writing material for Bob Hope. My first year on Burnett we not only won the Emmy, we knew it in advance.

That particular year the Academy tried to do something different. They announced winners in the different categories of writing — variety, sitcom, and so on. However, those "winners," they pointed out, would only be "nominees." Only one overall winner would be selected at the telecast to win the Emmy for writing. It was unusual, it was confusing, and it was controversial.

People objected to this and many of the stars said they wouldn't attend if this wasn't changed. So the Academy relented. They told all the "nominees" that they would now be Emmy winners and, in addition, there would be an "overall" winner for writing. So that's how we knew in advance that we would win an Emmy. (Incidentally, the Academy hasn't tried that since.)

As I was getting dressed in my rented tux, Bob Hope called. "I need a few things by tonight. . ."

I said, "Bob, I'm just getting ready to go out the door."

He said, "Where are you going?"

I said, "To the Emmys. I won an Emmy."

He paused for a bit, then said, "OK, here's what I need by tomorrow morning. . ."

Going Down?

(Martha)

One of the very first sketches I wrote for a Bob Hope show was a shampoo commercial parody that took place in an elevator. I remember how exciting it was to walk into the NBC studio that day and see that elevator set. Bob Keene always did a great job on the Hope sets, and this was no exception.

However, when the writing staff returned from their dinner break that night, we found the set for my sketch in the process of being torn down. The taping had been running long and cuts had to be made. My elevator piece was one of them. Nothing personal. It was just getting late.

I sat there and watched as the stage crew tore down the elevator section by section, piece by piece, nail by nail (ripping out my heart in the process).

As disappointing as that was, my pain was shortlived because the sketch was used in a later show starring Ann Jillian and Danny Thomas. I learned a valuable lesson that night, too, about working for Bob Hope. When it comes to material, this comedians' comedian never throws anything away. It stays in his files and sooner or later, he'll end up using it. And if he doesn't, then it just gives Milton Berle that much more to steal from.

You Get What You Pay for

(Gene)

Once in awhile the writers could almost get even with Hope. We were about to do a show in Sweden, a command performance for King Gustav. We had the first rehearsal at NBC in Burbank before we left.

All of the stars who were going to be on the show sat around a table reading the script. Hope turned to me at one point during the reading and said, "Gene, let's get a better joke there."

So I ad-libbed a new joke.

Hope said, "No, I don't think so."

I tried another one.

Hope shook his head no.

I thought I'd give it another shot, so I threw another gag at him.

Finally, in front of all these stars, Hope said, "Gene, when we do a joke on my show, we like to have people know what we're talking about."

Now I knew he was kidding, but I went along with it. I slammed my script onto the floor, threw my pencil across the room, stood up and said, "Bob, now you're getting into more expensive comedy."

Food for Thought

(Martha)

At the NBC tapings, Bob Hope used to enjoy giving us rewrite assignments just before our dinner break. Either a line in a sketch needed changing, a talk spot needed to be punched up, or a new monologue topic had just broken in the news.

We usually ate across the street at Chadney's restaurant. The food there was delicious. . .or so we heard from the non-writers in our party. Frankly, I don't think the writers ever got to taste any of it. We ate it, but we never really tasted it. We were too busy working.

Throughout the meal, each of us would scribble one-liners on our beverage napkin, then tuck it away in our pocket. Somewhere between the entree and dessert, we'd have enough lines to take back to the dressing room and try to "sell" to Bob Hope.

Sometimes the jokes worked and sometimes they didn't. Once Hope read them and said, "You guys have got to start eating at a place with funnier napkins."

The Idea That Wasn't

(Gene)

One time we had some sort of problem on a TV show we were doing and we all met in Bob Hope's office at his house. Several of us writers sat around a long conference table — Fred Fox, Si Jacobs, Bob Mills, Martha Bolton, and I. We were all trying to come up with a solution to this one problem.

Finally, Fred Fox thought he had a brilliant idea. He pushed back his chair, got up from the table, and started telling us his premise. But not only telling it — he acted out all the parts. He was jumping around the room, playing the different roles, and really putting a lot of enthusiasm into it.

We listened intently.

When he came to his ending, we all just looked at him. The idea died. It went nowhere. It had no point. It just didn't work. None of us knew what to say. We were embarrassed for poor Fred.

Then Bob Hope looked at him and said, "Fred, next time, don't stand up unless you're sure."

Instant Replay
(Martha)

Besides his quick wit, another thing about Bob Hope that always impressed me was his memory. He could remember a joke you wrote that he told at a 1987 Friar's Club roast, and he'd wonder why you couldn't remember it, too.

Often, we'd receive telephone calls from Bob asking about material that was buried in our files. He'd guide us to the date and event, and not only recite the joke, but the ones on the same page with it.

Gene and I, and no doubt the rest of the writing staff, had a hard time remembering the jokes we wrote yesterday, much less ten years ago. But then, I suppose that's just one more reason why Bob Hope is the legend.

Familiar?
(Gene)

There was a time when one of our writers — it wasn't me — handed in some "old" jokes to Bob Hope.

Hope read a few of them and said to the writer, "These have the faint aroma of nostalgia."

A Golden Couple
(Martha)

For Bob and Dolores' 50th wedding anniversary (they were married on February 19, 1934 in Erie, Pennsylvania), all of the writers decided to give them a congratulatory plaque with each of our names engraved on it, along with a mocha ice cream cake (one of Hope's favorite flavors).

That afternoon, we met at the offices at his home, then — checking to make sure the coast was clear of the guard dogs — we proceeded across the yard to the main house and up to Bob's second story dressing area, where he was waiting for us. All Hope knew was that his writers wanted to see him. He might have thought we were going to hit him up for a raise.

When he saw us approaching with gift and cake in hand, he couldn't have looked more surprised or pleased.

Over the years Bob has received over two thousand awards and honors, but after opening the plaque, he commented that this would be one of his most treasured ones because it was from his writers.

He thanked us sincerely. . .then gave us our next assignment.

I guess he didn't want us to have nothing to do on the drive home.

Good Investment

(Gene)

That 50th anniversary celebration was the time Bob Hope took all of us on a tour of his grand home in Toluca Lake. It's a glorious place that seems to ramble on forever. The backyard is huge and has a well-manicured golf hole there for Hope's practice. I don't know how many acres the property covers, but the joke is that everyone who lives in Toluca Lake lives across the street from Bob Hope. The place is magnificent, clearly worth millions.

I asked Bob when he moved into this house.

He said, "When I first moved to California in 1937, we paid $38,000 for the place."

I said, "Gee, Bob, you must have doubled your money since then."

"I keep an earthquake
emergency kit in my house.
It's filled with food, water,
and a half a dozen writers."
Bob Hope

Chapter Three
You Want Us to Write About What?

From the Frying Pan into the Fire
(Gene)

Whenever I give a talk about working with Bob Hope, I always say, "I've been with Bob Hope since 1969 and I've loved every minute of it." When my wife's in the audience, she gives me a look that kind of says, "You've got to be kidding."

She's right. Like any other job, there are times when I don't love it. There are times when it's a nuisance, when it's irritating, when I flat out hate the job.

In Bob Hope's stage act, he used to sing a medley of songs, about traveling around the country — "Back Home in Indiana," "California Here I Come," and other songs like that. And every so often, he'd stop and do a one-liner or two about that part of the country. There were about twelve spots in the song where he would do jokes.

We writers worked on that song for several years, providing new jokes, changing gags, and so on. It wasn't our favorite bit, but we got it polished pretty well.

There was one spot that Hope was never happy with. It was

when he did jokes about Boston. Almost every night he'd call and ask for new Boston jokes. He'd say, "Everything else is going well, but the Boston spot is weak."

So we'd write more Boston jokes and he'd put them into the song and then call back. "It's still weak," he'd say. "It brings the whole song down."

This went on for several months. All of us dreaded this "do more Boston jokes" phone call. He'd always say the same thing:

"Get everybody to work on some Boston jokes. The other eleven joke spots play so well, but this one doesn't come up to them."

So the next time he phoned, I called all the writers and said, "Look, we have a problem here and we're all getting sick of it. Let's really dig in and get the boss some great Boston jokes and let's get rid of this thing once and for all."

And everybody responded. They wrote their tails off. They sent me their stuff and I sent it to Bob Hope.

Next day I called him and said, "What did you think of the Boston stuff?"

He said, "Boy, that was dynamite. That spot really went through the roof."

I was thrilled.

Then he followed up by saying, "You know what, though, Gene? That stuff is so powerful that now it makes the other eleven spots look weak. Get everybody to start working on them."

Is There a Doctor in the House?

(Martha)

As Bob Hope writers, we've grown accustomed to tight deadlines. Bob's been known to call us for one-liners from backstage just before he steps into the spotlight.

One of our tightest deadlines came when Bob gave us the assignment to write for a psychiatrists' convention where he was to be the entertainment. Talk about a comedy writer's dream. That topic was so rich with humor angles, it could almost write itself. But when Bob arrived at the event, he discovered there had been a mixup. It wasn't a psychiatrists' convention after all. It was a chiropractor's convention. Now, we had less than a half-hour to write an entirely different routine!

We did it, but afterwards it was us writers who needed a psychiatrists' convention!

Nice Writing

(Gene)

People often ask if we writers ever get jealous seeing Bob Hope get the laughs and the applause for material that we write. We really don't. First of all, Bob Hope developed that comedy character over the years. He has a funny persona and brilliant timing. That's the real money; we suit our jokes to that.

Second, it's a thrill and a privilege to write material and have the absolute best in the world stand up there and deliver it. How can you be jealous about that?

However. . .there was this one time:

We used to do a parody of the song "Applause, Applause." Every time Bob did a concert appearance we'd write new lyrics to that song. This was yet another song all of us writers were getting sick of.

Hope was doing a concert for the Ferrari automobile company. The CEO would be there for the performance. So Hope called me and asked me to work up some special lyrics just for him.

I worked on a few and called Hope back. He wasn't thrilled with the material so we discussed it on the phone, came up with a few more ideas, and I went back to work.

When I called later, it still wasn't right.

This back and forth continued for the best part of the day. I must have written 25 different verses of the song for this executive.

The next day, when I talked to Hope, I asked how the song went over. He said, "Oh, it was great. I went to a party with the CEO last night and I sang the song for him there. He was floored. He loved it. And he was really stunned when I told him I just wrote it that afternoon."

Which Came First. . .
The Chicken or Laying an Egg?
(Martha)

Most of the time, though, Bob Hope was good about calling and telling you when one of your lines played beautifully. I wrote an opener for his appearance at a Kentucky Fried Chicken convention. The line was, "I knew I was at a Kentucky Fried Chicken convention the minute I walked in here tonight. No one shakes your hand. They just lick your fingers."

Bob said the line brought down the house. Not satisfied to leave well enough alone, I asked him about another line that I had turned in, a line that had a reference to another fried chicken chain and its slogan.

"Oh, yeah," he said, the excitement in his voice waning. "Was that your line, too?"

"Uh. . .yes. . .I think so," I said, hedging.

"Well. I did it and the audience just stared back at me. I felt like I was giving a lecture."

We learned later that the chain mentioned in the joke was only regional, not national, and had no franchises in that part of the country, so the audience had no idea what in the world he was talking about.

Comedy Writing Lesson #265: If you don't want to lay an egg at a fried chicken convention, make sure your references are nationally known.

"I have an idea that will simplify taxes. Why doesn't Washington just print their money with a return address on it?"

Bob Hope

Let Him Get His Own Writers
(Gene)

During our 1983 trip to Beirut we traveled to all of our shows by helicopter. These were large military choppers that were quite noisy, so we were required to wear helmets and hearing-protecting headsets. It was difficult to communicate.

On the way to one show, Hope was sitting next to Vic Damone and I was sitting on the other side of the aircraft, facing them. Hope motioned for me to come over and asked me for my pad and pen. I gave it to him and he wrote on it, "Let's work on a new joke for Vic. The one he has isn't working."

I wrote on the pad, "All the jokes I wrote are working."

Hope took the pad from me and wrote, "You're lucky you are."

Figuring I'd been topped by Hope again, I went back to my seat and wrote a few new lines. I passed them over to Hope, who read them and shook his head no.

I tried a few more. They didn't satisfy Hope, either.

So I wrote a few more lines and passed the pad over to Hope. He motioned for my pen. I gave it to him and he wrote on the pad and passed it back to me.

It read, "Why are we busting our tails to make him a star?"

The script stayed the way it was.

Quick Change Artists
(Martha)

Being a Bob Hope writer meant varied assignments. One day we'd be writing song lyrics, the next day it'd be a funeral tribute or an acceptance speech for some award or recognition, the following day we'd be back to one-liners and sketches.

Sometimes we had to do all three in the same day.

Sometimes we had to do all three in the same morning.

I recall one particular morning when that happened. We already had a noon deadline to write jokes on several different topics. Around ten o'clock, we received another call to put that assignment aside and write a comedy song that Hope needed in an hour. Then, just as we began that assignment, we received another call to write a funeral tribute — which needed to be back to him in only fifteen minutes.

Lucky for us, and the deceased, we didn't get the three mixed up.

Too Windy to Land

(Gene)

Doing a show on location always presented its own unique problems. On one trip, we were flying out of Aviara, Italy, on our way to Lajes Field in the Azores. There were reports that it was quite windy at Lajes, but the captain of our aircraft told us, "Don't worry, Bob, I'm going to try to land."

When he left, I said to Bob Hope, "Tell him to either land or don't land. I don't like this word, 'try.'"

Hope said, "Do some wind jokes."

So I headed back to my seat and wrote about 30 to 35 wind jokes. I reviewed them with Hope and we selected several to put into that night's monologue.

Then I went back to my seat to sneak in a nap.

It turned out we couldn't land in the Azores because of the heavy winds, so we made arrangements to fly to Rota, Spain and do a show at the military base there later that night.

That's when Hope came to my seat and tapped me on the shoulder. I woke up to see him standing there with the pages of wind jokes. He tore them up and said, "Do some Spain jokes."

The Purple Heart of Comedy
(Martha)

When we weren't on location, the Bob Hope show was taped in Studio 1 at the NBC studios in Burbank, California.

Bob's monologue was a closely guarded secret, known only to the producer, Hope's cue card man, Barney McNulty, and perhaps one or two others. The writers didn't even know which jokes "made it" into the monologue until the night of the taping.

That's when we'd all stand at the side of the stage and listen intently for our lines. When we'd recognize one of our jokes, we'd wait to see if it got a good laugh or even applause, then we'd jab the writer next to us and beam with pride. If our joke bombed, we'd look at the other writers and just shrug. . .as if to say "Ummm. . .I wonder who wrote that one?"

Depending on how our jokes played, we'd either go home with bruised ribs or a sore elbow. Luckily, Bob kept us all fully insured. But we did have a time explaining those injuries to the ER doctors.

Traveling Man
(Gene)

Bob Hope wrote an autobiography in 1954 called *Have Tux, Will Travel.* That was the phrase that a lot of vaudevillians would put in their ads in the trade papers. Hope was, and always will be, a traveling man. I used to tell him that I know he's going to heaven because he's got enough miles to get him there on his frequent flyer program.

When Hope travels, others travel with him. I've flown around the world with him twice. We took off from Los Angeles, flew west, and landed in Los Angeles ten days later.

Hope had a writer, Norman Sullivan, who was with him from his first radio show.

A general once asked Hope to do a show for the troops stationed in a remote area of Alaska. The general said they needed a morale boost badly.

Hope called Norman Sullivan and said, "Norman, I'm going to Alaska." The implication was, "You're going, too."

Norman said to Hope, "I'll move your pin on the map."

I Wanna Thank. . .
(Martha)

Sometimes the wacky assignments led to some interesting developments. One time was when Hope asked us to write an original song for one of his specials.

We did.

When the fortieth Emmy nominations were announced, I received a telephone call from fellow writer Bob Mills.

"Did you read the nominations in the *LA Times* this morning?" he asked.

"No," I said. "Why? Did you get nominated?"

"No. But you and Gene did."

Our nomination wasn't for "Comedy Writing," but for "Original Music."

Bob Hope's call congratulating us came next. But Gene and I couldn't have been more surprised over the nomination. We had written the lyrics to a song called, "A Man Is Innocent." Bob Alberti wrote the music. It was a big production number from our show spoofing the Iran-Contra hearings. The premise was that Bob Hope had been caught selling jokes to other networks from the basement of NBC. There was an investigation and, in the song, Bob and his attorney, Tony Randall, insist that a man is innocent until proven guilty. Danny Thomas, Milton Berle, and Jack Carter played politicians on the investigating committee. The song involved the entire cast, and it really was a nice piece in the show.

We didn't win the Emmy, though. A number in a Julie Andrews Christmas special won. But since ours was the first category read that night, we had the rest of the evening to relax, enjoy the festivities, watch the other nominees sweat it out, and do what writers do best — look around the room and see what kind of free souvenirs we could take home.

Freebies
(Gene)

Collecting souvenirs — hats, T-shirts, coffee mugs — was always a big part of our road trips with Hope. Sometimes we worked harder at that than we did on the show itself.

On my first military trip with Hope we made an interim stop in a foreign country and I was a bit nervous. We were surrounded by non-English-speaking soldiers with automatic weapons, and I didn't know if they were on our side or the other side. I also noticed that the U.S. military people accompanying us seemed concerned.

I was eager to get out of there. We had to wait as they loaded us onto helicopters, seven people at a time. I was among the last group to go.

Finally, just as our group was about to board, one of our party said to one of the U.S. servicemen loading us onto the helicopters, "I like that patch you have."

The soldier said, "If you don't mind waiting, I can get you some."

So we waited, surrounded by either friendly or non-friendly people with guns, just so this guy could get a free patch. If I weren't afraid of causing a war, I would have jumped on this guy and hurt him.

More About Souvenirs
(Martha)

Working for Bob Hope over the years has given each of us a pretty extensive collection of souvenirs. Bob always sends us unique gifts and pieces of correspondence. For our thirteenth wedding anniversary my husband had Bob and all the writers sign a cue card with good wishes. It's one of my favorite mementos, along with a neon sign that was used in a sketch on the Iran-Contra spoof show we did.

On this show, Hope's office in the NBC basement had a McDonald's-like sign that said, "Over 3 million jokes served." On cue it changed to "4 million." Since it was from a bit I had written, Bob Mills worked it out that I could have the sign after the show. I can't exactly wear it around my neck on a chain, but it's a great souvenir.

Of course now, after another decade in Bob's career, it should probably be changed to "5 million jokes served."

Old Jokes

(Gene)

When we were doing a command performance at the London Palladium, celebrating the 25th anniversary of Queen Elizabeth's coronation, we booked another guest on the show. It was the reigning Miss World, who was from Sweden, I believe.

Hope told the writers to quickly come up with a "talk spot" that he could do with her. Gig Henry, Bob Mills, and I went back to the hotel to work on the routine.

Gig was hot. He had plenty of good jokes that we immediately typed onto the page. There was no straight line that Gig didn't have a punch line for. We finished the spot in no time, had dinner, and Bob Mills and I ran the routine up to Hope's room. Now Mills and I were newcomers at this time and Gig Henry was a veteran Hope writer.

When we handed the material to Hope, he read it over without much enthusiasm. He said to us, "I've done all these jokes before."

Gig had "remembered" most of those punchlines. They were jokes that had been used on the Hope shows before. And Hope never forgets a punchline.

Now we had a problem. We needed an entire new routine for the taping the next morning. All the writers agreed to meet in the lobby at 6 a.m. to come up with a new routine.

We met at 6 a.m. but we didn't have any work to do. I spent the night in the bathroom of my hotel room. I sat in the dry tub so that I wouldn't wake my wife, and wrote a whole new routine overnight.

Bob Mills met us in the lobby with material in hand. He had done the same thing. We now had two brand new routines for Bob Hope to select from.

Gig just smiled. He knew the "two new kids" would come up with material, so the veteran comedy writer got a good night's sleep.

"I can understand airlines
charging a baggage handling fee.
After all, my luggage usually ends up
going a lot farther than I do."

Bob Hope

Chapter Four
The Master's Voice

Sweet Dreams
(Martha)

Bob Hope has a habit of calling his writers at all hours of the day or night. Because of the different time zones he travels to, getting a call from "the boss" in the wee hours of the morning just goes with the job (it may even be in our contract).

Les White, one of Bob's former writers, got more than his share of these late night interruptions. So much so, that when Bob called his house one night well past midnight, Les' wife decided to play a little joke on Bob.

"Is Les there?" Bob asked, wide awake and ready to work.

Les' wife looked over at her husband sleeping soundly in the bed next to her and didn't have the heart to wake him up.

"No," she said. "He told me he was going to be with you tonight."

There was an uncomfortable silence, then Bob said, "Oh, yeah. Here he comes now."

I Just Called to Say I Love You
(Gene)

Bob Hope would call with assignments any time of the day or night. And whenever he called, he immediately told you what he wanted so you could get to work on it right away.

I was sound asleep early one morning when the phone rang. It was Bob Hope calling from Vietnam. I wrote for those shows, but I was under contract to "The Carol Burnett Show" at this time, so I couldn't get away.

I answered the phone and sure enough the voice said, "Hi, Gene. It's Bob Hope." I mumbled a hello.

He talked for quite a while about the show and the trip and whatnot. Then it dawned on me that he hadn't asked for anything. I was eager to get back to sleep, so I said, "What do you need?"

He said, "Oh, I don't need any material. They just installed direct dialing over here and I wanted to see if it worked."

Just Checking In
(Martha)

Bob Hope's telephone calls came so often, you worried if a day went by without hearing from him or the office. So naturally, one August when he decided to extend his vacation in Alaska another week or so, we didn't really know what to do with ourselves. We'd send each other funny faxes (I recall a picture of Elvis with changing captions making the rounds), and a few of us took advantage of the respite to begin writing books or screenplays. But without those daily assignments that we had grown so accustomed to, time passed slowly.

Time must have passed slowly for Bob, too, because one night I came home and found this message on my answering machine:

"Hi, Martha. This is Bob Hope. I know it's been awhile since you've heard from me, but I just wanted to call to let you know I'm still in the business."

Where There's Smoke, There's Jokes
(Gene)

Hope always had a way of letting problems roll off his back. They'd upset him, you know, but then he'd do a gag or two and just shrug it off and let it go away.

I was on the phone with him once and he got another call. He said, "Hold on, will you? I've got a call on the other line."

So I waited and waited but he never came back on. I hung up and later found out what the problem was. On the news, they reported that the house he and Dolores were building in Palm Springs had caught fire. It burned practically to the ground.

The next day, he called me and said, "Did you hear about the house?"

I said, "Yeah, I'm really sorry."

He explained that was why he didn't get back on the phone, he was tied up with that.

I said, "I understand. It's no fun to have a house burn down."

He said, "Do some jokes about it."

I couldn't believe it. I said, "Really? How can you joke about something like that?"

He said, "We're glad it happened before we moved in. We're glad no one was hurt. Besides, what else can you do? Now it's a big story, so we'll do some lines about it."

To Bob Hope, everything's a topic.

Is Anybody There?
(Martha)

It was always interesting to come home and listen to your telephone messages. You never knew what was going to be on that tape.

I remember one message in particular. It went something like this:

"Hi, this is Bob Hope. I'm trying to find my writers. Gene's off speaking somewhere. Mills is golfing. Si and Freddie are gone and just have their answering machine on. And you're probably out shopping. . . .Didn't I used to have a career?"

On My Phone, No Less
(Gene)

There's a touch of glamour in working for Bob Hope. And we relished that little taste of celebrity.

My wife and I vacationed in Northern California once and when I was checking out of the hotel there was a message that Bob Hope had called. The desk clerk asked, "Is that the real Bob Hope?"

I said, "Yes, but I've already checked out of my room. Is there a pay phone around?"

He said, "Here, you can use our phone here at the desk."

So I dialed and began talking to Bob Hope.

While I was there, another couple arrived to check into the hotel. When they walked up to the clerk and before they had a chance to say anything, he said, "Have you ever heard of Bob Hope?"

Confused, they said, "Of course."

The clerk pointed to me and said proudly, "He's talking to him."

Skeptics
(Martha)

Not everyone believes you when you tell them what you do. Once while I was eating at a local fast food restaurant, my beeper went off. It was Bob Hope trying to reach me. I asked the manager if there was a pay phone around and he directed me to one outside by the walkway.

I called Bob Hope and we talked over the assignment, the deadline, then proceeded to just chat for about twenty minutes. Unbeknownst to me, a line of people wanting to use the telephone had formed. When I turned and noticed them, I told Bob I was at a pay phone and was going to have to clear the line.

Hanging up, I turned to the man directly behind me and said, "I'm sorry, but that was Bob Hope."

He just glared at me and said, "Yeah? Well, thanks a lot, lady! You just made me fifteen minutes late for my call to the Queen!"

How Fast Is Fast?

(Martha)

Bob Hope has always wanted his material to be topical, up-to-the-minute. If it's breaking in the news, he has to be talking about it. So, naturally, we have to be writing about it.

To give you an idea of just how on top of events Bob Hope wants to be, when Southern California was hit with yet another early morning earthquake, two calls immediately came into our home. Being a Los Angeles Police sergeant, my husband got a call to work the disaster patrol. Being a comedy writer for Bob Hope, I got a call to start writing one-liners.

My call came first.

Movers and Shakers

(Gene)

As Martha said, we get our share of earthquakes in Southern California. When we do, Bob Hope always wants a few jokes about them.

He called early one morning right after a quake had hit. I asked him, "How'd you like the earthquake?"

He said, "I didn't. Any time my bed moves that much, I like to have something to do with it."

Quake Prediction
(Gene)

I was talking with Bob Hope at his house on a day following an early morning earthquake. He was petting his dogs and mentioned that they were acting strange the evening before the quake.

He said, "You know, they say that animals have a way of knowing when an earthquake is coming. . .and they can warn you of it."

I said, "I think you're absolutely right. Last night my golden retriever grabbed the car keys and drove to Arizona."

Off the Top of My Head
(Martha)

Bob Hope has a way of "getting" you when you least expect it. He's as quick with the quip as Clint Eastwood is with the draw.

One day he called to ask for some jokes about a certain late breaking news item. Usually, we hang up, go to work, then call him back with whatever we've managed to come up with. But this time, he just hung on the line, breathing and waiting for instant brilliance. My brilliance is more the crockpot type, so, trying to buy myself some more time, I began, "Well, just off the top of my head. . ."

"Oh, no," Bob said, cutting me off. "We're not going to go up there again, are we?"

We Don't Do That Here
(Gene)

When he was traveling, Bob Hope would often call with new assignments. If I was unavailable, he'd leave a message and I'd call him back collect.

One day I came back from lunch and found a pink telephone

message slip on my desk. It read "Call Bob Hope" and it left a phone number.

I dialed the number collect. The person who answered the phone said, "We don't accept collect calls at the White House."

Friends in High Places

(Martha)

Speaking of the White House, for Bob Hope's last television special, "Laughing with the Presidents," we had the opportunity to write for most of the living presidents. When it came time to fax my material to Washington to be given to President Bill Clinton and First Lady Hillary Rodham Clinton, my son happened to be on the telephone talking to his girlfriend.

"Son, you have to clear the line," I said. "I need to fax in some material for the Bob Hope show."

"Okay," he signaled. "Give me just ten more minutes."

"No, you don't understand," I said. "This is going to Washington. The President of the United States is waiting for this."

"Okay," he said. "Make it five."

Obviously, he's a Republican.

I'm On

(Gene)

Before fax machines became common, we would call our jokes in to Bob Hope. That's a tough assignment because you're reading these jokes and waiting for laughs. Sometimes you get one; other times all you get is, "What else have you got?"

I was reading a bunch of lines to Hope one time and getting no response. I just kept reading, and it was unnerving. Finally, I asked, "Are you marking these or what?"

He said, "Just keep reading them. Keep reading."

So I kept reading the jokes and not getting much recognition one way or the other. Then in the background I heard a band playing "Thanks for the Memory" and I heard a voice saying, "Ladies and gentlemen, Mr. Bob Hope."

Hope said, "These are good jokes. I gotta go now; I'm on," and hung up.

Now that's calling it close.

Keeping up with the Times

(Martha)

Getting Bob Hope to move up to the world of the fax machine wasn't easy. Writer Bob Mills was the one who finally persuaded him.

One morning, Bob Mills asked each of us to call and dictate that day's jokes to him. He typed them up, rushed to a print shop and had them faxed to Hope. Less than an hour after calling us with the assignment, a hotel bellman was knocking on Bob Hope's door, handing him a hefty stack of perfectly typed jokes. Bob was impressed. Usually, he'd have to write out the jokes by hand as we read them over the phone — often, as Gene said, just before he was to walk on stage.

Needless to say, as soon as Bob returned home, he bought a fax. So did all the writers. But it backfired on us. The half-hour or so we thought we were saving in drive time, we now had to spend writing even more jokes. No matter how hard we tried, we just never could outsmart him.

"If they had co-ed dorms when I went to school,
you know what I'd be today? A sophmore."

Bob Hope

No Hello
(Gene)

Any time Bob Hope was traveling and discovered some interesting local topics, he'd call us writers to get right on it. "I'll call you back in half an hour," he'd say.

We'd write as much as we could and be ready for his call.

When he'd call back, he'd never say "Hello" or "How you doing?" or anything like that. You'd pick up the phone and Bob Hope would simply say, "Thrill me."

Miscommunications
(Martha)

Sometimes when Bob called, you weren't home so you'd have to get your assignment from message takers. Like the time my youngest son, Tony, wrote the following message on a napkin that he left on the sink: "Bob Hope's going to the doctor tomorrow and needs jokes."

Now, my initial response was, that's a strange assignment. But we've had strange assignments before. Like the time we had to write jokes for an aerial display from a helicopter flying over his Palm Springs home. We've also had to write one-liners for his golf foursomes and dinner parties, but never for his doctor's visits.

I wrote the jokes, but thought I'd better check it out before turning them in. So, I called Bob. It turned out the real assignment was that he was receiving an honorary doctorate and needed jokes.

That was one time I thought seriously about hiring a secretary — or firing a son.

Click. . .Dial Tone
(Gene)

Children can get you into trouble.

A few years ago my wife and I decided that our children were old enough to stay home alone while we went out to dinner. The restaurant was close by and we thought the kids would be fine. We did caution them not to tell anyone they were alone. "If anyone calls," I said, "Tell them Daddy's in the shower and take a message."

So Bob Hope called from New Orleans.

My daughter, as instructed, said, "Daddy's in the shower. May I take a message."

Bob Hope said, "Tell him it's Bob Hope calling. I'll wait for him to get out of the shower."

Now my daughter had no idea what to do. We hadn't given her a "Plan B." So she hung up.

Hope called back when we got home from our dinner. He gave me a writing assignment, then said, "Who answered the phone earlier?"

I said, "My daughter."

He said, "Have a little talk with your daughter. Tell her I'm a big star and you don't hang up on big stars."

Cleanliness Is Next to Unemployment
(Martha)

Spouses can get you into trouble, too. One Christmas, mine decided to surprise me with a housecleaning service. It was a nice gesture.

On the day the housekeeper came I had a pressing assignment due, so while I worked on it upstairs, she cleaned downstairs. Being the dynamo that she was, by noon she was ready to start cleaning upstairs. I decided that was the perfect time for a break, so I asked what she'd like to eat and went to get us some fast food.

I hadn't been gone that long, but when I returned, I went upstairs to get my assignment. All I had left to do was type it up and call it over to Hope's. That's when I discovered she had taken every single stack of paper cluttering my house and placed them all into a box the size of a washing machine. It did make the house look a lot better, and yes, she was just doing her job, but now my assignment was somewhere in the middle of about 14,000 pieces of paper and had to be called in to the Hope office in about twenty minutes.

I searched the box frantically, then gave up and just wrote new lines. After phoning them in, I called my husband and said, "Next year, Dear, just buy me a robe."

Have Yourself a Merry Little Christmas

(Martha)

Being a veteran of vaudeville, Bob Hope hardly took a day off. He worked weekdays, evenings, weekends, and most holidays. Once in awhile he'd give us writers a day off, but he didn't really want your brain vacationing.

I remember coming home from last minute shopping one Christmas Eve and playing back the messages on my answering machine. After a few season's wishes from family and friends, I heard Bob Hope's familiar voice coming from the machine.

"Hi, Martha," it began. "I know it's Christmas Eve and all, but I just wanted to say that while you're sitting around tonight drinking eggnog and opening Christmas gifts with your family, just remember . . .keep thinking, keep thinking."

"The stores are very crowded this Christmas. It's the first time I've ever been bumper to bumper when I wasn't in my car."

Bob Hope

Happy Holidays
(Gene)

Hope used to tell a story about Eddie Cantor. He gave his writers an assignment and one of them complained. "But, Eddie, it's Thanksgiving Day."

Cantor said, "So What? Thanksgiving doesn't start until 2 o'clock."

The Other Side of Hope
(Martha)

But every Bob Hope phone call didn't have to do with work.

Several weeks after my mother passed away from lymphoma, Bob Hope called just to see how I was doing. No assignment. No deadlines. Just heartfelt concern.

He and Dolores had already sent a floral cross to the funeral, and Bob, who was scheduled to be out of town that day, had sent along a personal message to be read at the services. But now, several weeks later, when everything was seemingly "business as usual," he was checking in with me. Though it had been decades since her passing, he shared with me how difficult his own mother's death was for him. "Losing a mother is one of the hardest things we have to go through," he said.

Out of all the times I've spoken with Bob Hope on the telephone, that conversation is one of my most cherished. It wasn't about business or the latest breaking news. It was just two friends talking about life, about loss, and about laughing again.

Chapter Four
Another Fine Mess. . .

You're Going
(Gene)

Bob Hope did his Vietnam Christmas shows for many years. When those ended, he didn't travel to many military locations for awhile because there were no trouble spots to travel to.

Then problems broke out in Beirut in 1983 and Hope was going to go there and do another Christmas show. The producer asked me if I would like to go to Beirut.

I said, "Well, I don't know if I'd like to or not, but I'll go."

Because of the logistics of this show — it would be done totally at sea — the Department of Defense limited the number of people who could travel with the show. Hope was going to take one writer.

We didn't know if it would be Bob Mills or me.

We did our regular Christmas show at NBC. Sunday evening, after the show was completed, all of us writers went into Hope's dressing room to say goodnight and recap the show a bit.

As Hope was leaving he stopped — I was standing by the doorway — looked me in the eye and said, "Pack."

That was Sunday evening. That's when I knew I was leaving for Beirut on Tuesday morning.

I Want You to Like Me

(Gene)

Right before we left for Beirut, Bob Hope asked me to pass on an assignment to the other writers. I missed one of them. Bob Hope never liked to miss out on material, so he was upset.

He called this writer, and the writer immediately called me.

He asked me to call Hope and verify that I had not given him the assignment. So I did.

I confessed my oversight to Hope. He was still a little miffed, but he appreciated my honesty and said, "Well, that's all right. I just hate to not get material, you know. And thanks for calling."

"Well, I wanted to call and square things with you," I said. "I don't want to be led into a war zone by a guy who's angry with me."

Where Are the Other Writers?

(Gene)

We did leave for Beirut on that Tuesday morning. This was my first military trip with the Bob Hope troupe, so I was very much in awe of the whole thing. We had a big press conference and send off at the military base we departed from.

When we boarded the Navy DC-9, I settled into my seat. After we took off, we were not in the air more than five minutes when Bob called me over and told me to look out his window.

I did, but didn't see anything extraordinary.

He said, "Look real good."

Still I didn't see anything special.

I said, "What am I looking for?"

He said, "If you look real close, you can see Bob Mills on the first tee."

Look Into My Eyes
(Gene)

On a flight from Los Angeles to New York, I sat in the second row of the tourist section of the plane. Bob Hope and the cast sat in first class. There were a couple of desks up there with seats on either side. Hope was seated on my side of the plane, facing the rear. There was a wall between the first class and tourist sections.

I was seated next to a gentleman I had never met before. He was hired for this trip. We introduced ourselves and chatted awhile. Then Hope switched sides of the plane. So I got up and moved to the other side as well.

Every time Hope switched sides, so would I. We did this several times. My seatmate was confused. He said, "What are you doing? Why do you keep switching seats?"

I explained to him that I always wanted to keep that partition between me and Mr. Hope. I knew that if he could see me across the aisle, he'd put me to work.

While I was saying this, Hope switched again, and when I turned around, he was looking right at me. He motioned for me to come up to see him.

Sure enough, he said, "I have a few things I want you to work on."

I worked for the rest of the flight.

He Could've Worked for the FBI
(Martha)

Bob Hope had a talent for tracking down his writers anywhere and at any time. We've been called during trips to Disneyland, church services, banquets, speaking engagements, doctor's visits, dentist's visits, Sunday drives, vacations, you name it.

Bob Hope even found me once while I was chaperoning my son's class on a field trip to the Santa Barbara mission here in Southern California. My beeper went off right in the middle of the Chumash Indian exhibit, and I had to leave the group to find a telephone. When I returned, I discovered our class wasn't where I had left them. They had moved on with the tour and it took me over an hour to find them. It was the first "missing parent" incident in the history of the school.

I didn't get detention, but they didn't ask me to chaperone too many times after that.

Incarcerated

(Gene)

At rehearsals for the command performance we did for Queen Elizabeth II, I sat in the audience while Bob Hope was going over some of the gags we wrote.

One in particular — one of mine — got groans from the people watching the rehearsal.

Hope reached into his pocket, took out some keys, and threw them to Bob Mills, the writer who was sitting next to me.

Mills caught them and said, "What are these for?"

Hope said, "Take Perret to the Tower of London."

I Know What the Queen Likes

(Gene)

Just before that command performance for Queen Elizabeth, we were rehearsing the monologue in the lounge of the Palladium Theatre.

Barney McNulty was flipping the cue cards as Bob Hope was giving them a last quick readthrough. He came to one joke about "nappies" — the British word for diapers — and the Queen's new grandchild.

Hope said, "Take that joke out."

It was a joke I'd written.

I said, "Bob, why are you dropping that joke? It's funny."

He said, "It's too rough for the Queen."

I said, "No, it's not. The Queen will love that joke."

Hope said, "Do you really think so?"

I said, "Of course."

He took the cue card from Barney and handed it to me. He said, "Then you do it."

Then he added, "Remember, she still has the power to behead."

Comedy in Good Taste

(Martha)

Delivering the material to Bob Hope in person wasn't always the safest thing to do. But it wasn't his secretaries who were threatening; it was his guard dogs.

Bob had two huge dogs on duty twenty-four hours a day. This was in addition to the security guards. I guess he didn't want Milton Berle sneaking into his joke files without an appointment. The only problem was that the dogs guarded the joke vaults from everyone — even the writers.

One afternoon while I was delivering my material, Snowjob, Bob's beloved white tank with fur, walked up to me, sniffed the pages of one-liners in my hand, then bit me on the foot. Apparently, he didn't like some of the jokes.

When word of this canine review reached Bob, he felt so bad, he sent me a telegram. It said, "Dear Martha, please come back soon. I'm ready for another hors d'oeuvre. Love, Snowjob."

The scar's faded now, but I still have that telegram. And yes, I did rewrite the material.

Killers

(Gene)

One show we did in Hawaii was a major operation for the writers on location. Normally, a show would be written well in advance and the writers at the site would handle only an occasional new line or minor rewrite.

For a number of reasons, this particular show required almost a total rework from page 1 on. At one point, as we finished a page an assistant would pick it up, photocopy it, get it to the performers, and come back up to our room to pick up the next page we had written. We were working that close to the taping deadline.

Bob Hope called one evening and said, "I'm taking you guys to dinner. I'll meet you in the lobby."

We met him at the lobby and walked to his limo. Hope asked the driver how far the restaurant was.

He said, "Oh, about a mile."

Hope said, "Let's walk."

I said, "Bob, it's a mile in the limo. When you're walking, it's three miles."

We walked and it was more like three miles.

We strolled through a part of town that was full of tattoo parlors and strip bars. With Bob Mills walking on one side of Hope and me on the other, people assumed we were bodyguards.

The strange thing is that when Mills and I realized this, we began to walk with a little swagger. You know, like, "Yeah, we're bad, man. . .we're bad."

Passersby must have been saying to themselves, "These guys don't look tough, but Bob Hope can afford the most vicious bodyguards in the world. These guys could probably kill you with one flick of the wrist."

We told Bob that everyone thought we were his bodyguards and asked if he felt safe.

Hope said, "I sure do. If any trouble starts, you guys will bad joke them to death."

In-Flight Safety Instructions
(Gene)

I was very naive about my first military trip with Bob Hope, the trip to Beirut. I knew that we'd be traveling around by helicopter. I pictured a glamorous flight over the Mediterranean in something that looked like a television traffic helicopter — just me and a pilot hovering peacefully over the water.

It wasn't like that at all.

Before we boarded our first helicopter, a Marine handed me a beat-up life vest and showed me how to put it on. Then another handed me a helmet with protectors to muffle the chopper's noise.

We boarded a big old helicopter that could carry forty of us, plus all our equipment. Glamorous it wasn't. We sat on canvas seats along the sides of the craft. I must have looked scared to death because Bob Hope looked at me and laughed. Then he leaned over and whispered, "You wanted to go into comedy."

I was a little apprehensive. But I wasn't terrified, until a Marine got up to give us our "safety instructions."

He was a short guy, but tough-looking. A real Marine.

You know the way flight attendants on commercial airlines recite the safety instructions pleasantly and with a big smile? This guy barked them at us like orders.

He said, "Should we crash on land. . ."

I turned to my leader, Bob Hope, and said, "Crash?"

The Marine went on. "Wait for all violent motion to cease."

I said to Hope, "Violent motion?"

"Then gather at the nose area of the aircraft." He continued, "Should we crash on water. . ."

I said, "Another crash?"

He said, "Wait for all violent motion to cease."

"More violent motion?"

"And inflate your life vest and swim to the nose area of the aircraft."

We hadn't had our first helicopter ride yet and I'd been through two crashes with violent motion.

Then our Marine grabbed a gun and leaned out the side of the craft as we took off.

I turned to Hope and said, "I guess we're not getting a snack on this flight, either."

I'm in Somebody's Scrapbook

(Gene)

When I traveled to Beirut with Bob Hope, it was one of the greatest Christmases of my life. It was inspiring to see how humor provided such a morale boost to the troops serving there.

For me, the trip was also a little bit humbling. As the writer, I traveled with the cast everywhere we went. And we did all of our shows at sea, moving from ship to ship by helicopter.

When our chopper would set down on the deck of a ship there would be hundreds of Marines and sailors waiting for the doors to open. Out of our chopper would step Bob Hope, Vic Damone, George Kirby, Cathy Lee Crosby, Ann Jillian, Miss USA, Brooke Shields. . .and me.

Guess who didn't get mobbed?

I almost got pushed overboard about four times in the rush to get to Bob Hope and the girls, to get pictures and autographs.

The USO, who sponsored the trip, gave us all white satin tennis jackets. They were to identify us as part of the Bob Hope troupe, not military. My jacket was a beautiful thing. It had an emblem on the breast, while on the back was a huge caricature of Bob Hope and red, white, and blue letters that read, "Bob Hope USO Tour, Beirut, Lebanon." I wore it everywhere.

On Christmas Eve, the cast flew to another ship to do a show that wasn't being televised, so I didn't have to go along. I waited on the USS *New Jersey* for the next helicopter back to our home ship, the USS *Guam*.

A young Marine all decked out to go back to the fighting onshore came over to me and said, "Can I have my picture taken with you?" I was delighted.

I said, "Sure. That's what we're here for."

He showed another Marine how to use the Instamatic. When he came back to me, I gave him my biggest smile and put my arm around his shoulder.

That was Christmas Eve, 1983. To this day, I'll never forget what he said to me.

He said, "No, no, no, man. Turn around."

All he wanted was the picture on the back of my jacket.

Your Autograph, Please

(Gene)

It's humbling being a writer surrounded by celebrities. During that Beirut trip, I came back with the cast to our home ship, the USS *Guam*, after a particularly harrowing ride across the Mediterranean in a small boat.

When I came onboard the *Guam* with the cast, a crew member approached me with a rolled-up poster. It was a picture of the ship and he had gotten it autographed by most of the stars on the show.

He asked me, "Would you sign my poster?"

I said, "I'd be happy to."

As I was getting out a pen, he said, "What do you do on the show?"

I said, "I'm one of the writers."

He said, "Well, sign it anyway."

"I go for a short swim every single day.
It's either that or buy a new golf ball."

Bob Hope

Fifteen Minutes of Fame. . .or Thereabouts

(Martha)

Sometimes our "humbling" was in front of a large audience — like the entire nation.

When the staff from "A Current Affair" called to ask if they could interview the Bob Hope writers, we were excited. Most of us usually prefer to stay behind the scenes, but once in awhile it's fun to step in front of the camera.

We all met ahead of time to "rehearse," to coordinate who would tell which story, etc. We wanted to be prepared. "A Current Affair" was a relatively new show, but it had already garnered a large, national audience.

The piece was taped at fellow writer Bob Mills' home. Everyone looked great. A few had bought new shirts. One or two got a haircut earlier that day. I even spent $50 on a professional make-up job (it was the lowest bid I could find).

Gordon Elliott conducted the interview, and I think we told him every Bob Hope story we could think of. Si Jacobs told his stories, Fred Fox told his stories, followed by Gene Perret, Bob Mills and me.

The cameras were rolling for about forty-five minutes. The lights were melting my make-up, but I didn't care. We were going to be on national television.

They told us the date that the show would air, and we all sat glued to our respective television screens, awaiting our fifteen minutes of fame.

Our fifteen minutes turned into about fifteen seconds. We were upstaged by a piece on Bob Hope's joke vaults.

The vaults *are* interesting. One contains 52 large file drawers filled with jokes dating all the way back to 1934. Not unlike a bank vault, this vault is encased in walls of cinder block and has a door six inches thick, held by three one-inch deadbolt locks. The other vault is filled with personal appearance monologues and unused gags. If the house ever goes up in flames, the jokes will survive.

So none of us could really blame Gordon Elliott for giving more air time to the joke vaults than to us, but for that one day, at least, we had to have been better-looking.

Gotta Go

(Gene)

When we were taping a Christmas special from the Persian Gulf, we were invited to a party at the United States Ambassador's house in Bahrain.

The military warned us about Bahrain. They told us not to take pictures of women who didn't want their pictures taken. They also told us to behave ourselves — to not smoke anything we shouldn't be smoking. And not to steal anything. They cut off fingers or hands for theft.

Bahrain was also susceptible to terrorist attacks because security was not as stringent there.

Before the party, we went on a shopping trip in the marketplace in Bahrain. Bob Hope rode with the Commodore, and I went with the Captain of our ship. I thought I'd be safe with him, but he was a bit nervous about traveling through Bahrain. That made me even more frightened.

While we were shopping, it became necessary for me to use the men's room. I didn't know where it was and since I didn't speak the language, it was difficult to ask.

The situation became critical. I had to go. If they cut off fingers for theft, I wondered what they did for the offense I was about to commit.

Finally, I saw a men's room and rushed over to it. I tried the door but the place was locked. As I jiggled the doorknob, a guard came over, gun drawn, yelling at me in some foreign language.

I somehow motioned that I just wanted to use the men's room, and he kept motioning for me to go into a store. When I did follow his direction, the storekeeper gave me a set of keys to the restroom and told me, in English, to return them when I was through with them.

Thank goodness, that problem was solved, my life was saved, and now I never go anywhere without a traveler's phrase book.

Nice Party, Except. . .

(Gene)

We were warned about the tough laws and punishment in Bahrain. We were reminded that Bahrainis cut off various parts of your body for different offenses. And we were accompanied by armed guards everywhere we went.

The U.S. Ambassador's house, where we attended a party, was surrounded by soldiers with automatic weapons. . .and they were all alert.

It was intimidating.

The party was also attended by many dignitaries, including members of the diplomatic corps. It was very elegant and the food and drink was plentiful and fine. Nevertheless, I was glad when the party ended so we could get back to our aircraft.

When the van delivered us to the airport, I was one of the first ones to board the C-141. I wanted to fly away and leave our armed guards behind.

As I walked down the aisle, I saw Bob Hope sitting in his compartment on the plane. He motioned me in and said, "How'd you like that place?

I said, "It was a beautiful home."

He asked, "Did you enjoy the party?"

I said, "It was a great party, Bob, except for one thing."

"What's that?"

Behind my back I pulled my hand up into the sleeve of my jacket. Then I held the sleeve out to Bob Hope with the hand "missing," and said, "You steal one lousy ashtray. . ."

Hope fell out of his seat and slammed his hand on the floor laughing. It may have been the biggest laugh I ever got from Bob Hope.

Remembering When

(Martha)

It's fun to get together with other Bob Hope writers and recall stories. We've done it at Hope parties, for television and radio interviews, and for several of his own television specials.

One of our most memorable round table discussions was for an event sponsored by the Academy of Television Arts and Sciences celebrating Bob Hope's 94th birthday, and covered by Entertainment Tonight. Moderated by Hal Kanter, the panel included Melville Shavelson, Mort Lachman, Larry Gelbart, Sherwood Schwartz, Gene Perret, and me.

A favorite story of all of ours was shared by Sherwood Schwartz. It happened when Schwartz was a junior writer for Bob Hope. Bob loves ice cream, and it was the unspoken "duty" of the junior writer to get it for him.

After having to leave Hope for several years to serve in the armed forces, Sherwood returned to Bob with a carton of ice cream in hand. He rang his doorbell. Hope opened the door, saw the ice cream, and simply said, "What took you so long?"

At the Academy celebration, Sherwood handed Bob another carton of ice cream. Bob Hope laughed harder than anyone — and kept the ice cream.

"President Kennedy invited me to
stay at the White House.
I guess he figured after the
Bay of Pigs, what's another ham?"

Bob Hope

Chapter Five
Friends of Hope

Is This Any Way to Rehearse?
(Gene)

We got word during our taping of a show at Pope Air Force Base in North Carolina that President Reagan was going to "drop in." The President was at some function in Alabama and would land at Pope AFB on his way back to Washington to wish Bob a happy birthday.

Hope said to the writers — Bob Mills and I were on location — "Write a little vaudeville bit for the Prez and me."

I said, "But he'll be here in about an hour."

Hope said, "Then you'd better get to work."

Mills and I wrote out about a three- or four-minute talk spot between Bob Hope and President Reagan. We presented it to Hope and he said, "Let's go rehearse."

He took the sheets of paper and us into the Secret Service headquarters at the base. From there they dialed the President aboard Air Force One, and Bob Hope and Ronald Reagan rehearsed their comedy routine with Mills and me listening in and making changes.

The President objected to one line and I threw in an ad-lib that he accepted.

We made the changes in the script and had the routine put on cue cards.

Later, Air Force One landed at the base. The President rode up to the stage in a limousine, rehearsed with the cue cards, went on stage and did his bit with Hope to a rousing audience reception.

Then he got in his limo and went back to Air Force One and continued on his way to Washington. Once again, he left show business for politics.

Your Place or Mine?

(Gene)

When we first heard that the President was coming to Pope Air Force Base, the entire atmosphere around our facilities changed. First "the suits" arrived. I suppose they were Secret Service personnel doing a reconnaissance of the area.

Then the dogs arrived. They sniffed everything in the area that was sniffable.

Then the uniforms arrived. In addition to the suits, the Secret Service also has uniformed officers who patrol the area where the President is or will be.

And our movements were restricted. We had to remain in areas that were already "swept" or "cleaned" or whatever term they use for meaning that security had approved it.

When the President arrived, an official came over to Bob Hope's dressing room, where he and I were going over some aspect of the show. This gentleman asked Hope, "Do you want to rehearse with the President in your trailer or his?"

Hope said, "Whatever is most convenient for him."

The man suggested, "His place is secured; yours isn't."

Hope said, "Then we'll rehearse there."

The gentleman left. Hope turned to me and said, "Why should I mess up my trailer for a lame duck?"

Presidential Reprieve

(Martha)

When Bob Hope turned ninety years of age, NBC celebrated his birthday by airing the Emmy-Award-winning special, "Bob Hope — The First Ninety Years." Dolores Hope later threw a private birthday party at their home.

Anyone who was anyone was at that private party. Legendary entertainers and notables such as Jimmy Stewart and General William Westmoreland attended, as did former presidents Gerald Ford and Ronald Reagan.

Gene and I chatted briefly with President Ford. Afterward, we found ourselves wishing we had asked him to pose for a picture.

Having missed that opportunity, I wasn't about to let another one slip by. As my husband, Russ, and I were walking to the dining area (which was under a huge white tent set up in the back yard), I noticed that Ronald and Nancy Reagan were walking right in front of us.

Somehow I got up the courage to ask the President if he'd mind posing for a picture with me. He graciously agreed. The President and I posed, my husband snapped the shot — but unfortunately, the flash didn't go off. It was dark, so I knew the picture wouldn't turn out. But how do you ask a former President of the United States for a second chance? I didn't have to.

"Would you like to try it again?" Mr. Reagan said.

I couldn't believe it! He was giving my camera a reprieve! I quickly posed again, we smiled, my husband snapped the picture — and again, the flash didn't go off. Feeling sick to my stomach, I thanked the President, and we all proceeded on into the tent.

I had the roll of film developed, and just as I feared, the picture didn't turn out. But I went ahead and had it enlarged and framed and hung it on my wall. To anyone else, it just looks like a blank frame. But I know it's me and Ronald Reagan!

The topper to this story is that, when I later received the Ambassador Award from Media Fellowship International, I happened to mention this story in my acceptance speech. Afterward a man approached me and asked,

"So did you ever get that picture?"

I said, "No. I had my two chances and I blew it."

He said, "Well, maybe I can help."

Then, reaching into his pocket, he pulled out his business card and handed it to me. It was Michael Reagan, the President's son.

The next week I received a telephone call from the President's office. Ronald Reagan invited me and my entire family to have our pictures taken with him. They must have taken twenty poses — the President with me, the President with my husband, each son with the President, the whole family with the President. Needless to say, the pictures turned out a whole lot better than my original one ever would have, even if the flash had worked.

We were showing those pictures to some friends the other day and they asked, "Is that really Ronald Reagan?"

My husband nodded, "Yeah, but he's with five cardboard figures of us."

Give Us Something to Write About

(Gene)

When Martha and I spoke with former President Gerald Ford at Bob Hope's 90th birthday party, I said, "Mr. President, I have to thank you. You've provided a lot of joke material for us writers. Each time I hand in a page of gags to Mr. Hope, you're mentioned."

He laughed and said, "You have to write more of those golf jokes. You know when I go on speaking engagements, I always tell a few of Bob's jokes on myself."

I said, "Well, you're welcome to them."

"But write some new ones," he said. "I need them."

Gerald Ford turned to walk away and I called after him. "Mr. President. . ."

He turned back.

I said, "Hit somebody, will ya?"

Comedy Has No Age Limits

(Martha)

On one of the shows, when George Burns was performing a sketch with Bob Hope, George flubbed one of his lines. The audience laughed and the director had them start over.

When George got to that same line, he flubbed it again. Once again, the audience laughed — not at him, but with him. It seemed the audience was enjoying watching "show business" in action, getting a front row seat to those "Take Ones" and "Take Twos."

After "Take Three" and "Take Four," the audience was in hysterics. George and Bob were having a good time, too.

Finally, when "Take Five" didn't work because of another Burns flub, George turned to the audience and said, "I'm ninety years old. What do you expect?"

The laugh he got with that could be heard almost all the way to the NBC commissary.

Career Move

(Gene)

Two writers, Fred Fox and Si Jacobs, used to work with George Burns and were now on the Bob Hope staff. One night, while we were all having dinner during a break at an NBC taping, I asked them, "How come you guys signed on with Bob Hope?"

Si Jacobs explained, "We wanted to get with a younger comedian."

"There are 86 golf courses in the Palm Springs area, and Jerry Ford never knows which one he'll play until his second shot."

Bob Hope

We Turn Up in the Strangest Places

(Martha)

When Bob Hope's and Melville Shavelson's book, *Don't Shoot, It's Only Me*, hit the shelves, the Hope staff did a show about it. The cold opening for the show featured Bob autographing copies of the bestseller at a bookstore. Standing in line waiting to talk to Bob were Dolores Hope ("I heard you were in town") and Henry Kissinger (comedic lines delivered with his accent were hysterical).

If you look closely, you can see someone else standing in the line — Hope writer Si Jacobs. But I don't think he had a book in his hand for Bob to sign. I think he was just dropping off more jokes.

Outtakes

(Martha)

When the late great Sammy Davis, Jr. guest-starred on our show, he and Bob were scheduled to do a dance number together. It was sure to be the highlight of the entire program. Sammy, though, missed one of the steps and he and Bob collided. Sammy just smiled and said, "Sorry, Bob. I only have one eye and it was looking the other way."

It brought down the house.

Delayed Reaction

(Martha)

Phyllis Diller guest-starred on one of our shows, which was being taped at a packed football stadium. Phyllis did her usual hysterical monologue and the audience roared. The only problem was, in that type of venue, the laughter took awhile to make it to the stage. So, for a few seconds after each joke, Phyllis had to stand there and listen to deafening silence.

After her set, she turned and walked offstage, quipping to Bob and others who were standing nearby, "Comedy isn't for the outdoors."

Geronimo!

(Gene)

I stood with Bob Hope and Phyllis Diller once watching the famous cliff divers perform at Acapulco. They'd scale the precipice, pausing half way for a prayer. Then, when the wave came in, they'd dive into the ocean.

Bob Hope turned to Phyllis Diller and said, "Isn't that incredible?"

Phyllis said, "Not to me it isn't. My blind dates do things like that all the time."

Tongue-Tied

(Martha)

Usually, we were proud to claim our lines. We'd call each other on the telephone and read our favorites. We'd beam at the readthrough if a joke of ours went over well. Once in awhile, though, a line just didn't work and you'd wish you didn't have to claim authorship.

Such was the case with one of mine when Garth Brooks guested on our show. Our assignment was to write a talk spot for Bob and Garth. Talk spots were short, conversational bits between Bob and his guest stars. The line I wrote for Bob to introduce Garth was "Garth Brooks is one of the most sought-after performers in show business today." But Bob kept getting tongue-tied on my choice of words. What repeatedly came out was "Garth Brooks is one of the most sawed-off performers in show business today."

Music Hath Charm

(Gene)

When we did the show in Tahiti, it seemed as if every night there was a party for us. All the parties had the same food. It was like a Tahitian picnic. They had the Tahitian version of potato salad and that kind of stuff. Of course, every event featured Island music. After a while that can get a little cloying.

One night we were having a party at a hotel. Bob Hope sat at the first table with our host. We writers sat at the table next to that.

We ate, the party went on, the music continued and it was a nice time. During a break in the action, Jonathan Winters got up to go for a little walk and he came over to our table. He knelt down between two of us writers, put his arms around the backs of our chairs, and whispered to us, "I don't know about you boys, but musically, this is the most exciting night of my life."

Teed Off

(Martha)

When Mr. T guest-starred on one of our shows, there was a problem with his contract. I believe it inadvertently hadn't been signed by our producers, and he wasn't going to walk on stage until the matter had been taken care of. . .or something like that. Whatever it was, I'm sure he had a point.

Unfortunately, this was also the show on which the senior writers decided I should start getting practice going over the lines with the stars. So, they sent me to "sell" Mr. T on a line change.

I found Mr. T at the side of the stage. Bob was already on stage performing, and it was almost time for Mr. T's cue. So I quickly approached him. I was both excited and nervous. This was a big moment in my career. It could only mean one of two things — my fellow writers had gained confidence in me and trusted my negotiation skills, or they didn't want to give up their seats in the green room.

Now, I'm tall, but Mr. T was taller, a lot bigger, and definitely not interested in a line change. When I introduced myself, he just started pacing and shouting things like, "I don't want any writers! I want my contract taken care of! Don't want any writers! Just the writer who's going to take care of this contract!"

I stood there, paralyzed with fear. It may have all been part of his stage persona, but I was buying it hook, line and sinker. Finally, I managed to get out the words, "Uh, maybe I'll take care of this later," then turned to walk away. When I did, I saw the rest of the writing team, standing off to the side, laughing hysterically. They had been standing there watching the whole thing!

The contract matter got taken care of and Mr. T went on to perform his lines as only he can. It was a great show. But to this day, the writers say they've never seen anyone's face as flushed or eyes as big as mine were that moment.

And You Are. . . ?

(Martha)

One story that Gene would prefer to forget happened at a dinner for former Secretary of State Dick Cheney. We were guests of Bob and Dolores Hope, and since they were seated at the head table, Gene and I felt we should go over and let them know we were there.

Dolores was the first to notice us approaching.

"Oh, look, Bob," she said, turning in our direction. "It's Martha Bolton and. . .What's-His-Name."

We both knew Dolores was only putting Gene on, but I've tucked that story away in my collection and enjoy reminding him of it as often as possible. As you can see, though, it still didn't get me top billing on this book.

Now He Knows How Hope Feels
(Martha)

Here's a story that might balance out the previous one and keep getting me invited to Gene's Christmas party.

The NBC show celebrating Bob Hope's 90th birthday was an incredible event. It was strictly invitation only and black tie. Everybody who was anybody was there. It was held on my son, Russ', 19th birthday, so Linda Hope arranged seats for my whole family. Working on the Hope staff was always family friendly.

Now, I'm going to brag a little about my co-author. Most television shows hire a comedian who comes out and "warms up" the audience just before the show. Since this was a special event, and since Gene had quite a speaking career going, Linda asked him if he'd do the pre-show talk. Gene agreed, then saw the guest list. In the audience would be Karl Malden, Telly Savalas, Ginger Rogers, and a host of other Hollywood notables, television bigwigs, military brass, and a former President or two. But Gene was terrific.

Oh, he was a little nervous before the show. (I know that because he didn't even notice Raquel Welch when she stopped us to ask directions.) But when he stepped out onto the stage, he was a pro. He had everyone, including Bob and Dolores Hope, in stitches telling classic Hope stories.

So if Bob Hope ever really retires, who knows. . . ?

Chapter Six
Now That's Clout

One of a Kind
(Martha)

Gene and I both have written for a variety of comedians. But Bob Hope is definitely in a class by himself. Who else would ever call and say, "I'm having a fleet of naval ships named after me. Do some jokes, will ya?" Bob has had buildings named after him, airplanes named after him, medical centers, cultural centers, and who knows what else.

I remember when the City of Burbank renamed the street in front of NBC Bob Hope Drive, we got the assignment to write some jokes for the dedication ceremony. Bob used a line I had written for his opener. Walking up to the podium, he looked out at the hundreds of press and well wishers gathered there and said, "It's an honor to have a street named after me. . .especially since all the oceans were taken."

He Calmed the Seas
(Gene)

There was one time when I was in awe of Bob Hope. I also wanted to wring his neck.

We were doing a Christmas show off the coast of Beirut in 1983. We did all of our shows at sea so we travelled to the different ships by helicopter. The Navy warned us that they wouldn't fly us after dark because we were in a war zone. Having lights on the chopper presented too easy a target for the enemy and not having lights on it was too dangerous for flying. So once it got dark, we were stranded.

That's what happened when we were on the USS *New Jersey*. We were waiting for Bob Hope. The helicopters were ready to take us back to our base ship, the USS *Guam*. But Hope kept delaying the departure. Finally, our helicopter just took off without us.

The Captain of the *New Jersey* sent us back to the *Guam* in a small craft. He said, "It may be a little choppy, but you can tell whoever is driving (or whatever it is you do with a small craft) to go at whatever speed you want."

It was a harrowing trip because the sky was pitch black over the Mediterranean, the sea itself was like ink, and it was rough. After about an hour's ride we got back to the USS *Guam*.

Now we had to disembark. The waves seemed like they were at least six feet high at times. The *Guam* had a floating dock over the side, and our craft was tied up to it, but the waves kept throwing us all over the place. At times, the dock was five or six feet above or below our craft. When they would come together they would slam hard against each other. If you fell into the sea, you'd be crushed by the impact.

The sailors helped all the women onto the floating dock and up the stairs to the *Guam*. I was worried about them, but I was more concerned about Hope.

Eventually, it was just him and me left on the small craft. Hope stepped to the edge of the ship, humming jauntily. When it was time for him to cross over, the seas calmed, and he just walked across like he was strolling along the fairway.

Now it was my turn and the waves kicked up. It seemed like they were making up for that moment of calm when Hope stepped across. The sailors held onto my arms and warned me not to try to jump (not walk — jump) across yet.

I was being tossed around and looked up at Hope going up the stairs to the *Guam*, still humming serenely.

I would have cursed him if I wasn't so busy praying for my own survival.

You Shoulda Seen It
(Gene)

Bob Hope is a powerful man. Sometimes he thinks that the rest of us have that same sort of power.

In Sweden, we were all invited to a party that was being held in the room where everyone banquets after they award the Nobel Prizes. I was very much looking forward to seeing the place.

Right before the luncheon, Hope called with some NAFTS (that was our acronym for his requests for material because they always started with "I Need A Few Things. . .").

I said, "I'll get on it right after the luncheon."

He said, "You don't have to go to that lunch. Stay here and work on the gags and have them ready for me this afternoon."

So I missed the party.

When I called Hope to see if I could run the new material up to his room, he asked, "What did you think of that place, huh?"

I said, "I didn't see it. You told us to stay here and work on the script."

He said, "Oh boy, it's great. Have someone run you over there to take a look at it."

Bob Hope can call someone to run him over to Stockholm's City Hall for a personal tour. I don't think I could.

We'll Set Up Here, Thank You
(Gene)

Power wasn't something Bob Hope wielded or flaunted; he simply had it. Here's an example.

We were setting up to shoot on location at Mann's Chinese Theatre in Hollywood. The cameras and lighting were arranged, the set was in place, extras were on hand, the cue cards were available. All we needed was Hope.

When he arrived, he didn't like the location. Moving it would take at least an hour, but Hope wanted it moved, so it would be moved.

However, this was only going to be a short take, so we had no portable dressing rooms or offices on site. That didn't bother Hope. He walked down Hollywood Boulevard to a movie theatre. The staff followed.

Hope walked into the theatre, which was open for business, selling tickets and admitting people to the shows. He found a comfortable chair in the lobby and sat down.

The theatre manager rushed over. I thought he was going to ask us to leave. Instead he welcomed Mr. Hope and asked if there was anything he could get him. We all accepted some cold drinks.

From that moment on, that theatre lobby was Hope's headquarters for the day's shooting.

Take Me to Your Leader

(Martha)

On one of the many Bob Hope shows where we spoofed television, I wrote some special "breaking news" spoofs. Lines like: "We interrupt this program just to remind you that we have that power" and "We interrupt this program to inform you there's a better one on another station."

Bob wanted to include the bits in the show. So much so that when we discovered there was a problem with clearing the lines, he went straight to the top. Evidentally, the phrase "We interrupt" couldn't be used because the public might think it was a real bulletin.

Bob took the issue to the top of NBC in Burbank, then all the way to the top at NBC in New York. He may have come close to getting it approved, but it was still a no-go. The public safety had to take precedence over a laugh.

It did make me feel pretty good about Bob Hope as a boss, though. When he believed in your work, he *really* believed in your work.

Take Your Pick
(Gene)

Sometimes you didn't dare laugh at the funny things that happened.

In Bermuda, we had taped a segment of the show in the market square. As we were driving back to our hotel, we got jammed up in traffic. Bob Hope rolled down the window to get a little fresh air.

One of the street vendors came over to the limousine and put her head right in through the window. She was nose to nose with Bob Hope.

She had a big smile with lots of teeth missing. You could tell she was delighted to be in the presence of a show business legend. She glanced around at the rest of us in the car.

She looked at the driver, who was a huge man, about 6 foot 5, weighing almost 300 pounds. Then she eyed Bob's make-up man, who was in the front seat on the passenger side; he had a large, black moustache. Then she looked at me. I was sitting on the opposite side of the back seat. I'm bald with a grey beard and moustache. Then she looked back at Bob Hope.

She looked around at the four of us once again, then said, to Bob Hope, "OK, which one is Bob Hope?"

This Is Bob, You'd-Know-My-Voice-Anywhere, Hope
(Martha)

Once when Bob Hope's secretary was trying to book him a room at a hotel, she ran into a skeptic too. The hotel reservation clerk didn't believe her and there was absolutely no convincing him. The telephone conversation went something like this:

"I'm calling for Bob Hope. He'd like to book a room there."

"C'mon, lady, I don't have time for this."

"I'm serious. I'm calling for Bob Hope. He'd like to book a room."

"Is this what you do all day? Pull pranks on people?"

"Look, would you like me to get Bob Hope on the phone and have him tell you himself?"

"Yeah, sure. Why don't you just do that?" he snapped.

The secretary put the hotel clerk on hold, then buzzed Bob Hope. She explained the trouble she was having and asked if he'd mind straightening the guy out. Bob obliged. He picked up the line and simply started singing, "Thanks for the memory. . ."

The clerk hung up on him.

Chapter Seven
Backstage with Bob Hope

The Root of the Matter
(Martha)

If Bob Hope is anything, he is the consummate performer. He's from the old school, a former vaudevillian who believes first and foremost that "the show must go on."

I remember talking to him after a performance one night. He had had a root canal earlier in the day and still, he went through with the show.

"The Novocain hadn't worn off yet and I kept slurring my words," he laughed. "They probably thought I was drunk."

"Didn't you tell them you had dental work done?" I asked.

"No, no," he said, emphatically. "You never do that. You want laughs, not sympathy."

That was one thing about working for Bob Hope. It was like taking a crash course in comedy, and you were learning from the master. He knew how to handle an audience. But then again, I've had root canals. I think I would've gone for the sympathy.

Dogsitter
(Gene)

Bob Hope brought his dog with him on one show we did on location. He brought his pet out to me and said, "Would you take him for a walk?"

I said, "Bob, I don't walk dogs for a living."

He said, "Yes, you do. Read the small print in your contract."

Singing Dogs
(Martha)

For one of our Christmas specials, taped on location at their Palm Springs home, Bob and Dolores were scheduled to sing "Silver Bells" with their family dogs seated by their feet. It was a beautiful picture — Bob and Dolores all decked out in their holiday finery, and the dogs sporting big red ribbons against all that shocking white fur. The scene was so festive, the Hopes made it their Christmas card that year.

Unfortunately, though, every time Bob started to sing the song, the dogs would begin to howl. He'd sing a note, they'd howl three. It turned out to be one of the funniest spots in the whole show. The dogs were such a hit by the time they finally walked off the set, Bob couldn't help but quip, "It's okay. Let 'em go. They're late for their audition for 'Lassie Unplugged.'"

Coming In on a Wing and a Prayer
(Gene)

Bob Hope called me one time and said, "C'mon over and have lunch with me. I want to talk over the projects for the coming year."

It was about a half-hour drive from my home to his house in

Toluca Lake. As I was pulling in the driveway, Bob Hope was driving out. We both stopped, put down the windows, and he said, "Park your car and take a ride with me. I have to go pick up Dolores."

Mrs. Hope, it turned out, was flying in on a small, private plane from Palm Springs. Dolores Hope works with Catholic charities all over the country and many of her friends are in the clergy.

So Bob and I got to the Burbank airport and waited behind the chain link fence. The plane landed, taxied up, and the steps came down. The first two people off the plane were Catholic priests. Then Mrs. Hope came down the steps. Then four more priests.

Bob Hope kind of nudged me and said, "I don't know why she just doesn't buy insurance like everybody else."

Private Show
(Martha)

After having written for Bob Hope for about a year (and after they had talked with him numerous times on the telephone), my sons asked if they could meet him.

I had to drop off some material at his house anyway, so I called Bob to inquire if he'd like to meet a couple of nine-year-olds and an eleven-year-old. He said, "Sure."

With a Grandma Moses painting and numerous portraits of Bob on the wall behind them, my sons, Russ, Matt, and Tony, sat on the sofa, waiting. Bob's voice entered the room first. You see, Bob is always singing — not really a song, just melodic sounds that keep his voice in good condition. We could hear those sounds as he walked down the stairs from his bedroom, through the kitchen, down the hall, and finally into the play room.

I introduced the boys to him, and to my amazement, he sat down and proceeded to tell them joke after joke after joke. Right there in his home, Bob Hope was doing his act with an audience of four. No wonder the man's a show business legend. He knows it's never too early to start hooking tomorrow's audience today.

Keeper of the Purse

(Gene)

Hope was always famous for keeping an eye on the budget. When you're working in television with major stars and major egos, you do have to be on guard. The budget can run away with you.

A bunch of us were sitting in Bob Hope's suite in Stockholm, Sweden, working on the script for the special we were doing there. Mrs. Hope came in to say goodbye to Bob.

"Where are you going?" he asked.

She said, "Just out to do some shopping."

When she reached the door, he yelled after her, "Don't buy anything you can get at K-mart."

On the Right or On the Left?

(Martha)

On one of our television specials, a sketch called for Bob Hope to play Gorbachev. Thanks to Don Miranda's incredible make-up skills, he ended up looking remarkably like the Soviet leader. The only problem was his forehead birthmark. It was on the wrong side.

Bob insisted it was correct and, anyway, there wasn't time to change it. Of course, Bob was going by his reflection in the mirror, and in the mirror, the birthmark was on the correct side, where it would be if you looked at Gorbachev on TV. But on camera it was on the wrong side, because that wasn't a mirror image.

None of the viewers wrote in to complain about it, though. Maybe they thought we had done it on purpose — for a laugh.

"Ohio's changed a lot since I was a kid.
For one thing, it's a state now."

Bob Hope

What Might Have Been

(Gene)

Bob Hope always enjoyed a joke — even when it was on him.

My writing partner, Bill Richmond, and I went to meet with Bob Hope at his house. We were sitting in the "playroom." It's a large room with a table and chairs set against a bay window where we could overlook the backyard. The yard, of course, was spacious, elegantly groomed, and had a practice golf hole back there.

There was a break in our meeting and Hope was telling us about his early years, in radio. One of his regular golfing buddies was a man who owned a company that made the boxes for Hope's sponsor's product. But the guy hadn't been playing lately. Hope asked him, "How come you're not out here playing golf?"

The guy said, "I really can't get away. We're so doggone busy that I can't get the time to play golf."

Hope knew that if this gentleman was working so hard making containers, Hope's show was selling product for the sponsor. He told his agent to get some big money.

The sponsors (and I forget which company it was but it's one that is very well known and prosperous today) came back and offered him five percent of the company.

Hope said, "No way. I want money. I want cash."

So he got a good deal, but, he said to us, "Can you imagine what would have happened if I had taken five percent of that company back then?"

We sat there in this very luxurious home overlooking a glorious garden and Bill Richmond said to Hope, "Geez, Bob, you could have been on Easy Street today."

Starstruck
(Martha)

When it came to fans, I don't believe anyone could be as accommodating as Bob Hope. A friend of one of the staff members attended our office Christmas party one year. After greeting everyone and enjoying the refreshments, Bob and several of us, including this friend, retired to the back room to watch the football game in progress. All during the game, the man couldn't take his eyes off Bob Hope. It was as though he couldn't believe he was actually in the same room with this comedy legend. What made it so awkward, though, was the fact that the man was sitting in the chair right next to Bob and leaning just inches from Bob's face.

Bob Hope didn't say a word. He didn't ask for privacy or a little breathing room. He just watched the game and let this man stare at his pores as much as he liked. To the rest of us in the room, watching all this was quite comical. To Bob Hope, it was just another day.

We All Have Off Days
(Gene)

I love the way Bob Hope can be fair about everything and honest about himself.

We were planning a show and he called me about a potential guest — a young comic whom I had seen several times and wasn't crazy about.

Hope asked, "What do you think of him?"

I didn't want to put the guy down, but I also didn't want to praise him because I didn't really want him on the show. So I said, "Well, Bob, I'll tell you, I've seen him a number of times and sometimes he's very good. At other times he's not that thrilling."

There was a pause at the other end of the phone and Hope said, "Gene. . .that's all of us."

I Wish I Made That Kind of Money
(Gene)

While I was working with Bob Hope, I also did several speaking engagements each year. Hope knew about them; in fact, they were written into my contract. However, once in a while they would conflict with my duties on the show.

When I arrived back from one engagement, Hope had me paged at the airport and told me to report directly to the Hope offices before going home.

I did.

When I walked into the office, I knew that Hope was a little peeved that I had delayed the meeting. He said, "You were out speaking, huh?"

I said, "Yeah."

He said, "Do your act for us."

I said, "I can't, Bob. It's all your material."

He said, "You're not funnier than I am, are you?"

I said, "No, but what I can't understand is that I tell a lot of the same jokes you do, and yet I only get paid half of what you get."

Hope was working then for about $50,000 an appearance.

In my dreams I got half of what he got. The trouble is I always woke up before I could cash the check.

Gone Fishing
(Martha)

The only vacation the Hope writers could count on was when Bob took a week or so off every August to go fishing in Alaska. It was then, and only then, that we could turn our beepers off, let our fax machines cool down, and give our typing fingers a much-needed rest.

That rest was cut short one summer, though. Bob had only been gone a few days when our phones started ringing again. When asked why he had decided to come home so early, he simply said, "Fish don't applaud."

How Are You Going to Get Home?
(Gene)

I sat with Bob Hope in his dressing room before a show we were scheduled to do in Paris. Some executives with the companies sponsoring the telecast came in to chat with Hope.

Bob was telling them a story about a joke he had used many years ago. As he was telling them the year, he turned to me and said, "Were you with me then?"

I said, "No, I didn't join you until 1969. But I'm very surprised by that story, Bob. I didn't realize you did jokes before I came on board."

He sneered and said, "Funny ones."

Can You Top This?
(Gene)

During the limousine ride to the outdoor ampitheatre in Honolulu, where Hope was appearing, Bob and I were trading show business stories. I told him a funny tale about the comedian I worked for when I first began as a comedy writer, Slappy White.

I forget what the story was, but Bob Hope answered with a story of his own. It was about a time he was a guest in Buckingham Palace and he saw a few dogs roaming about. He reached down and petted them and asked their names. A voice gave him the names of the pets. It was Queen Elizabeth II.

I said, "Bob, if every time I tell a Slappy White story, you're going to answer with one about royalty, we might as well just ride in silence."

Now That's Research
(Martha)

When my son, Matt, was in junior high, his teacher gave his class the assignment to write a biography on a famous person. My son chose Bob Hope.

After doing some initial research on Bob's life and career, he asked me if I thought Bob Hope would let him interview him. I was a little leery, after all, it wasn't *Newsweek* or *Time*, it was a junior high school report, but, I thought, why not give it a try.

So Matt called the office and Bob Hope immediately got on the line and let my son ask him questions for about twenty minutes! Pretty impressive for a show business legend.

Matt finished the report and turned it in. He only got a "B." But not without an explanation. His teacher told him he would have given him an "A" had he not "made up" that story about interviewing Bob Hope.

I've Seen Better on Pianos
(Gene)

Sometimes Hope would call writers' meetings without much notice. "Get here and get here immediately." At one of these hastily called meetings, Bob Mills arrived wearing shorts. He apologized for being a bit late. Hope ignored the apology, stared at his legs, and said, "Does the Red Cross know about those knees?"

It's About Time
(Martha)

Bob Hope has always been known for his precise timing. But not only on stage. During one of his USO tours to Vietnam, the crew got to see just how remarkable Hope's timing is.

The troupe had just wrapped up a show and were preparing to take off for their next show in Saigon when the cue card stand collapsed, creating a huge mess. Barney McNulty, Hope's cue card man, had to put the cards back in order (and we're talking hundreds of cards), so the departure was delayed by ten minutes or so.

What nobody realized at the time was that a Vietcong bomb had been set to go off upon Bob Hope's arrival at the hotel. It did, but that ten-minute delay saved his life. Today, whenever Bob Hope recalls the story, he can't help but add, "Saved by the idiot cards. . .again."

Bob's Favorite Audience
(Martha)

Bob Hope is probably most beloved for all he's done for our military. Presidents have honored him, and recently, Congress named him an honorary U.S. veteran for his half-century of entertaining our troops all over the globe. He's the first person to be so honored.

Whatever the public has seen Bob Hope do for our guys and gals in uniform, there's plenty they aren't even aware of. I've read thousands of letters that Bob has received from GIs, and most of them are thanking him for some act of kindness he showed to them personally. He either sent them the harmonica or fruitcake they asked for, let them borrow some of his material for their own "shows," or called their mother or father when he got back to the States to let them know that they were all right.

One of my favorite letters was from a soldier who had walked with his company all day in order to reach the Bob Hope USO show that night. When they arrived exhausted, they found the area swarming with so many GIs, they couldn't get close enough to the stage to see or hear anything. So they left and started heading back.

Bob Hope heard about the incident and, when the show was over, got several of the stars into a jeep, drove out and met them on the road, and put on a private show just for them.

Chapter Eight
Thanks for the Memories

Fond Memory
(Gene)

Every once in a while something happens that you wish you could just press between the pages of your scrapbook and keep forever, like a dried rose from the school prom.

Bob Hope had asked me to do some special lyrics for a guest star he was appearing with. These requests were always tough for me. I find it hard to write any song lyrics without using the word "really" three or four times in the song.

I wrote the material, though, brought it over to Hope's house, and handed it to him. He didn't open it. He just held it in his hand and said, "Is this brilliant?"

I said, "Bob, if I could write brilliant song lyrics, would I be writing comedy?"

He paused and said very seriously, "Gene, I think you would."

It was a great moment for me. Still is.

In a Class by Himself
(Martha)

Bob Hope once remarked, "If I had my life to live over again, I wouldn't have the time." It's no secret Bob Hope has led an incredible life. He's entertained presidents, kings, queens, four-star generals, and has performed with nearly all the major stars of this century. Bob Hope has risen to the top of every facet of show business — vaudeville, Broadway, radio, television, and movies. His talent is legendary, his fans are legion.

He's also a pretty nice guy. In more than fifteen years of having written for Bob Hope, I can honestly say he's never spoken a single unkind word to me. I'd venture to say most of America can't report that about their bosses. And after watching him during our hundreds of meetings at his house, dressing room conferences at NBC, dinners, banquets, birthday celebrations, and whatever else popped up on his calendar, I've learned a lot about the man. I've seen his eyes tear up whenever he talks about his memories of entertaining the soldiers, and visiting the sick bays on his USO tours. I've watched him interact with lifelong friends he's loved and respected — Lucille Ball, George Burns, Phyllis Diller, Jimmy Stewart, Milton Berle, Danny Thomas — while being equally at home with today's young stars.

But what's intrigued me the most about Bob Hope is how he has never taken his own good fortune for granted. His excitement for show business, life and laughter has never once waned.

One afternoon while I was dropping off some material at his house, Bob was eager to give me a tour of his newly remodeled office. Dolores had done a beautiful job designing the changes and Bob wanted to show it off.

As he pointed out the various pictures hanging on each wall — the one of him with four living presidents, the one of him with the late John F. Kennedy, numerous photos of him with celebrities and international dignitaries — I noticed something interesting. It was almost as if he were on the outside looking in, as though he himself couldn't believe where his career had taken him and how much living he had packed into his 90-plus years.

Then, after Bob had described the final photo and we started to make our way down the hallway, he paused. Glancing back toward the memory-filled room, and in genuine awe and sincere appreciation for the life he had been blessed with, he flashed that famous Bob Hope grin and said, "It's something, isn't it, Martha? It really is something."

"Vaudeville is where I learned
my expert timing.
You know, to always duck
right after the punchline."
Bob Hope

Thanks for the Memory

Bob Hope would usually end his television specials with special lyrics to his theme song, "Thanks for the Memory." We thought it would be fitting to close our book the same way.

So, Maestro, music please

Thanks for the memory
Of calls throughout the night,
You'd say with delight,
"It's half-past two
And time for you
To wake up now and write."
We thank you so much.

Thanks for the trips we made.
Around the world we'd trot
To each trouble spot.
We'd never know
Where we might go
But thanks for all those shots.
We'd do it again.

Working for you was inviting
'Cause you made our lives so exciting.
Yes, you kept us constantly writing.
We wrote, we found
Jokes by the pound

So, thanks for just being you —
Our fav'rite boss by far,
Legendary star
From NBC
And peacocks to
Your golf games under par
We want the world to know how
Truly wonderful you are.

We thank you so much.